Canals

Diyan Leake

Heinemann
LIBRARY
Chicago, Illinois

Edited by Joanna Issa and Penny West
Designed by Philippa Jenkins
Original illustrations © Capstone Global Library Ltd 2014
Picture research by Mica Brancic
Production by Helen McCreath
Originated by Capstone Global Library Ltd
Printed and bound in China by Leo Paper Group

18 17 16 15 14
10 9 8 7 6 5 4 3 2 1

Library of Congress Cataloging-in-Publication Data

Leake, Diyan, author.
  Canals / Diyan Leake.
     pages cm.—(Water, water everywhere!)
  Summary: "In this book, children learn all about canals,
including different types of canal, how people use canals, and
how to stay safe near canals. The book also includes a world
map showing some of the most important canals in each
continent."—Provided by publisher.
  Includes bibliographical references and index.
  ISBN 978-1-4846-0451-9 (hb)
  1. Canals—Juvenile literature. I. Title.

TC745
386.4—dc23   2013039548

Acknowledgments

We would like to thank the following for permission to reproduce
photographs: Alamy pp. 5 (© Robin Weaver), 7 (© LOOK Die
Bildagentur der Fotografen GmbH), 10 (© idp canal collection),
11 (© Robert Harding World Imagery), 14 (© Chris Howes/Wild
Places Photography), 16, 23c (© Steven May), 17 (© David
Reed), 18 (© Barrie Neil), 21 (© Convery flowers), 22b (© Peter
Fakler), 22c (© idp canal collection), 23b (© Chris Howes/Wild
Places Photography); Getty Images pp. 6 (AFP Photo/Carl de
Souza), 12 (National Geographic/Jonathan Kingston), 19 (The
Image Bank/Jamie Marshall - Tribaleye Images); Shutterstock
pp. 4 (© Leonid Andronov), 9 (© Oleksandr Kalinichenko), 13 (©
Chris Jenner), 20 (© David P. Lewis), 22a (© Kevin Eaves), 23a (©
Irina Fischer); Superstock p. 15 (JTB Photo).

Cover photograph reproduced with permission of Alamy
(© Terry Mathews).
Back cover photograph reproduced with permission of
Shutterstock/© Oleksandr Kalinichenko.

We would like to thank Michael Bright and Nancy Harris for their
invaluable help in the preparation of this book.

Every effort has been made to contact copyright holders of
material reproduced in this book. Any omissions will be rectified
in subsequent printings if notice is given to the publisher.

006996LeoF14

Contents

Canals

Canals are waterways.

Canals are like roads for boats
and ships to go on.

People build canals.

Canals look like rivers, but they have straight sides.

Canals of the World

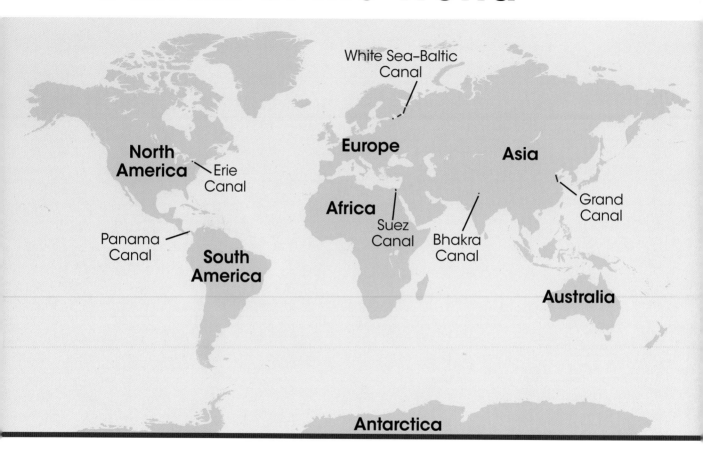

There are canals all over the world.

The Suez Canal is one of the biggest canals in the world.

Boats and Ships on Canals

Some canals are small. Boats travel through small canals.

Some canals are big. Ships travel through big canals.

Canals can join one sea
to another.

12

Barges carrying cargo go
through canals like this.

Where Do Canals Go?

Some canals go through the country.

Some canals go through
towns and cities.

Some canals have locks.

16

Locks are like steps going up
and down a canal.

Vacations on Canals

People take vacations on canals.

This vacation barge is in the country of India.

Having Fun on Canals

It is fun to spend time on a canal.

Stay safe! Always have an adult with you when you are near water.

Quiz

Which of these is a canal?

A

B

C

Answer on page 24

Picture Glossary

 **barge** flat-bottomed boat used on canals to carry people or goods

 **country** land away from towns and cities

 **lock** part of a canal with gates at each end for a boat to pass through

23

Index

Answer to quiz on page 22: Picture **C** shows a canal.

Note to Parents and Teachers
Before reading
Ask the children if they have ever visited a canal. Encourage those who have to describe what they did on their visit and what they saw while they were there. Find out what the children already know about canals. Do they know the difference between a canal and a river? Do they know what people use canals for?

After reading
• Turn to pages 16 and 17. Explain more about how locks work. Ask the children to suggest why they think locks are necessary in canals. Display photos or videos from the Internet that show locks in action.
• Find a map that shows the location of the Panama Canal. Explain how this canal changed how ships travel from the East coast to the West coast of the United States. Before the canal, ships would have to travel around the southern tip of South America to get from New York to San Francisco, for example. The canal cut out thousands of miles of travel by connecting the Atlantic and Pacific oceans. Ask the children to discuss how this would affect business and trade.